# The Family Dog

## Celebrating Our Favorite Relative

Linda Sunshine
& Mary Tiegreen

Clarkson Potter/Publishers
New York

Published by Clarkson Potter/Publishers, New York, New York
Member of the Crown Publishing Group, a division of Random House, Inc.
www.randomhouse.com

Permissions and photo credits appear on page 111.

CLARKSON N. POTTER is a trademark and POTTER and colophon are registered trademarks of Random House, Inc.

Printed in Singapore

Design by Mary Tiegreen

Library of Congress Cataloging-in-Publication Data
Sunshine, Linda.
    The family dog / Linda Sunshine and Mary Tiegreen.
        p.    cm.
    1. Dogs.    2. Dogs—Pictorial works.    3. Dogs—Literary collections.
I. Tiegreen, Mary.    II. Title.
SF 426.2 .S86     2003
636.7'0887—dc21                                        2002192460

ISBN 1-4000-4593-2

10  9  8  7  6  5  4  3  2  1

First Edition

This book is dedicated to
Daisy,
whose intelligence, joy, and happy spirit
were legendary.

♥

# dog people

Even before my own family had a dog, I was a Dog Person. In the cool north woods of Michigan, where we spent our summers, dogs were always around and, as an only child, these dogs were my companions and my cousins. Together we ran in the forest and dog-paddled in the lake, shared ice-cream cones outside the general store, and sat together in the dark by the glowing campfire. On clear, cool summer nights we would sit at the end of the dock under the bright dome of twinkling stars and wait for the

northern lights. Dogs are good at this since they don't mind the cold and they respect the perfect silence required for contemplating the universe. There we'd sit, just the two of us, cuddled up for warmth, the silence broken on occasion by the splash of a fish jumping for mayflies down the shore.

Over the years, I've walked with many dogs down the silent, solitary path beside the lake in search of a deeper connection to my life. While Shadow, our little black cocker spaniel, was fearless, Katie, our bearded collie mix, was timid and never strayed far from my side. Luger, my uncle's dachshund, was relentless in his quest for animals, large and small. With his nose in the air, he'd waddle down the trail covered in a carpet of brown pine needles, short legs scrambling over the thick roots of the tall white pine. Then, suddenly, he'd catch a scent and break for the woods, disappearing beneath the ground cover of ferns. Much later, we'd find him in a standoff with a chattering squirrel high up in a tree.

Susan's dog, Sherlock, a German shepherd–golden retriever mix, was bold and strong and would run ahead, tail held high like a flag, a brave scout leading the way. The most magnificent of them all was Daisy, our golden retriever, who loved to bound through the tall ferns and leap over fallen logs with incredible strength and beauty. She seemed to run for the sheer joy of running, and there was something perfect in that moment when she was free and full of life. Being there with her gave me a feeling of transcendence and grace.

The Dog People in my family prefer the company of most dogs to that of most humans. With dogs we experience an innocent and deep connection that one can rarely find with another human. Dogs seem to see into our souls and offer us kindness, devotion, and complete acceptance. We talk to them and sing to them and take them on rides in the car because we know they like the car. We carry their pictures in our wallets and select our clothing and furniture based on the color of their fur.

We Dog People love our dogs and cherish their lives in photographs and stories. Every dog may have a tale, but a dog needs a person to pass it down and keep the memory alive. Every one of our family dogs had a story. These well-worn legends outlived each dog and were told over and over until they were perfectly polished and smooth as a bone.

Long after Old Fritzie was gone, for example, my family told stories about how this bulldog chased the old Model A Ford all the way from town and swam across the lake to get to the camp before the family arrived.

Fritzie had originally belonged to my mother's cousins who lived down the street but apparently preferred my grandmother's cooking and decided to move into her household. For several weeks, cousin Francis would come over and bring Fritzie back home, but he'd made up his bulldog mind. They could take him home but he'd always return in time for Grandmother's supper. Finally, he won and settled into life with his chosen family. No one wanted to argue with Old Fritzie.

Then there was the story of Pete, a dog from my grandmother Nelson's farm. I always imagined Pete to be a dog who resembled Old Yeller. As my grandmother used to tell it, she was just a young girl when her father lent Pete to a man who needed a dog for hunting. The man returned without poor Pete, explaining he had lost the dog somewhere in the faraway woods. (As a child I always hated this part of the story.)

One month later—"almost to the day," my grandmother would say in a you're-not-going-to-believe-this voice, as if I'd never heard the story before—poor old Pete came hobbling into the yard, thin and bedraggled. He'd found his way back to his family through fifty miles of forest and farmland. "And I'll tell you one thing," my grandmother would always say, "if I'd had a tail I woulda' wagged it!"

Our family told stories about Maya and Pesa, who could pull a sled across the frozen Minnesota lake, and Perry, who would toss her kibble in the air and dance around before she would eat it. They talked about Schmidtty's terrifying encounter with a porcupine, and Daisy, who learned how to close the back door in exchange for a cookie. And, of course, there was Scoop, who ate three socks and a T-shirt in one sitting.

My uncle Bob, a dedicated Dog Person if ever there was one, always shared his life with at least one, if not three, dachshunds. Like most Dog People, he had, over the years, received numerous dachshund gifts, including glass figurines, sectional nut dishes, T-shirts, calendars, coffee mugs, refrigerator magnets, welcome mats, music boxes, collectible china plates, and a shish kebab set. And like most Dog People, he bored the pants off anyone willing to listen to endless stories of his dogs' superior intelligence, their singing talents (with a demonstration), and their skill at catching small pieces of sausages in midair.

I am grateful for every moment I've had with dogs—walking in the woods or fighting for space in the bed, playing hide-and-seek, sitting together under the stars. These moments have been special gifts of love, humor, and true devotion.

A wise Dog Person once described a perfect world as one in which "every dog would have a home, and every home would have a dog." This book celebrates that special world and the people who share it with their best friends and devoted companions.

Mary Tiegreen

*There are many families where the whole interest of life is centered upon the dog.*

Jerome K. Jerome
*Idle Thoughts of an Idle Fellow, 1889*

# What the dogs have taught me

We are pretty sure that we and our pets share the same reality, until one day we come home to find that our wistful, intelligent friend, who reminds us of our better self, has decided that a good way to spend the day is to open a box of Brillo pads, unravel a few, distribute some throughout the house, and eat or wear the rest. And we shake our heads in an inability to comprehend what went wrong here.

Merrill Markoe
*What the Dogs Have Taught Me, 1992*

*Dogs feel very strongly
that they should always
go with you in the car,
in case the need should arise
for them to bark violently
at nothing right
in your ear.*

Dave Barry

*Dogs will come when called.*
*Cats will take a message*
*and get back to you.*

Missy Dizick and Mary Bly
*Dogs Are Better Than Cats!*, 1985

# This dog could smell love

You always heard that dogs could smell fear; this dog could smell love. Whenever people were touching, embracing, kissing, she would be there, offering her front paw or nose for a similar embrace. She horned in on several moments a day. And there were times when David felt she was the most loved of the three of them.

Antonya Nelson
"Dog Problems"
*The Expendables*, 1999

## Asking for a pup

**O**rvie had more than a longing for a pup, he had a determination to possess one, gave his father and mother little rest from the topic, and did all he could to impose his will upon theirs. Their great question had thus become whether it would be worse to have a pup or to have Orvie go on everlastingly asking for one.

Booth Tarkington
"Blue Milk," 1934

# The rest of our lives together

On the Christmas morning of my eleventh year, as I stood walking a new Slinky from hand to hand, my little sister shrieked, "A puppy!" and a roly-poly wirehaired fox terrier pup came tumbling across the rug. My sister fell to her knees and scooped the puppy up, but I, stunned, dropped the Slinky and sank slowly to the couch. A dog. My dog. She was finally here. My parents, I told myself, will never regret this. Never will either one of them have to feed her, or walk her, or discipline her. Never will I give them any reason to say, "I'm sorry we ever let you have that damned dog." The responsibility kept me seated on that couch for a good long moment. In fact, it surprised everyone, even me, that I didn't rush to the dog as my sister had, but I was thinking, "We have the rest of our lives together."

Elisabeth Rose
*For the Love of a Dog: A Memoir,* 2001

# When my brother proposed a toast

**M**y brother had chosen the Atlantis [for his wedding] not for its sentimental value but because it allowed the various family dogs. Paul's friends, a group the rest of us referred to as simply "the dudes," had also brought their pets, which howled and whined and clawed at the sliding glass doors. This was what happened to people who didn't have children, who didn't even know people who had children. The flower girl was in heat. The rehearsal dinner included both canned and dry food, and when my brother proposed a toast to his "beautiful bitch," everyone assumed he was talking about the pug.

David Sedaris
"Rooster at the Hitchin' Post"
*Esquire*, September 2002

# In love with my dog

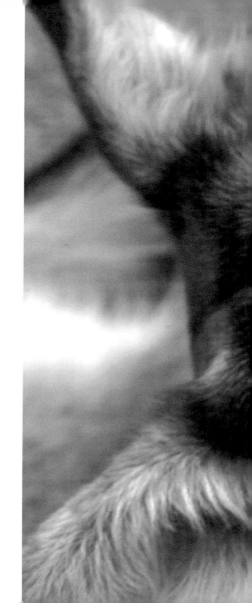

**I** have fallen in love with my dog. This happened almost accidentally, as though I woke up one morning and realized: Oops! I'm thirty-eight and I'm single, and I'm having my most intense and gratifying relationship with a dog. But we all learn about love in different ways, and this way happens to be mine, through a two-year-old, forty-five-pound shepherd mix named Lucille.

Caroline Knapp
*Pack of Two*, 1998

## Bessie loves him

**B**essie can be very kind, though she usually saves her kind side for children and animals. She has a little dog who belonged to someone in the neighborhood who didn't want him anymore. He's part Chihuahua and I don't know what else, and he has some nasty habits, but Bessie loves him. She never eats a meal without saving the best piece for her little dog. . . . If only I could get Bessie to be as sweet to people as she is to her animals.

Sarah and A. Elizabeth Delany
*Having Our Say,* 1993

*I feel the same spiritual comfort
holding a leash that others
feel holding a rosary.*

Susan Conant
*A New Leash on Death,* 1990

# Food

When I first got him I called him Gilbert, the name I still introduce him by. The only word he will always answer to, however, is Food, so I generally call him that.

Jack Alan
"From Pillar to Post," 1942

CODY

RITZY

BILLIKEN

ELTON

HAROLD

RUBY

COYOTE

DAISY

ARUBA

**SHADOW**

**BRUNO**

**MRS. MAGOO**

**SPARKLE**

**DUSTY**

# Names of dogs

N ames of dogs, to get back to our subject, have a range almost as wide as that of the violin. They run from such plain and simple names as Spot, Sport, Rex, and Brownie to fancy appellations such as Prince Rudolph Hertenberg Gratzheim of Darndorf-Putzelhorst and Darling Mist o' Love III of Heather-Light-Holyrood—names originated by adults, all of whom in every other way, I am told, have made a normal adjustment to life.

James Thurber
"How to Name a Dog"
*Good Housekeeping,* October 1944

# He wasn't about
# to respond

**B**ill would not be suppressed. Sometimes he would come when you called, sometimes not. But even when he did come he had this funny look on him, as if he was coming over just to find out why you persisted in calling his name when it had already been established that he wasn't about to respond.

Ethan Mordden
"The Complete Death
of the Clown Dog"
*The Company of Dogs*, 1990

*If a dog will not come to you after having looked you in the face, you should go home and examine your conscience.*

Woodrow Wilson

# Regardless of what they say

 man down in Texas heard Pat on the radio mention the fact that our two daughters would like to have a dog. And, believe it or not, the day before we left on this campaign trip we got a message from Union Station in Baltimore saying they had a package for us. We went down to get it. You know what that was? It was a little cocker spaniel dog in a crate that he had sent all the way from Texas. Black-and-white spotted. And our little girl, Tricia, the six-year-old, named it Checkers. And you know, the kids love the dog, and I just want to say this right now, that regardless of what they say about it, we're gonna keep it.

Richard Milhous Nixon
Comment after being accused of
accepting improper gifts, 1952

Dogs act exactly the
way we would act if
we had no shame.

Cynthia Heimel
1993

The great pleasure of a dog
is that you may make a fool
of yourself with him and not
only will he not scold you,
but he will make a fool
of himself, too.

Samuel Butler
*Notebooks*, 1912

*You can say any fool thing to
a dog, and the dog will give
you this look that says,
"My God, you're RIGHT!
I NEVER would've
thought of that!"*

Dave Barry

# One redeeming feature

**T**he dog's one redeeming feature was that when he heard someone pronounce the word *sit* he would sit. That fact brought Bundy a certain distinction, and the gratitude of many shop owners.

Wright Morris
"Victrola"
*The New Yorker,* April 12, 1982

# A number of dogs

M y home is a haven for one
who enjoys
The clamor of children and
earsplitting noise
From a number of dogs
who are always about,
And who want to come in
and, once in, to go out.

Ralph Wotherspoon
"My Dumb Friends"

# Our link to paradise

**D**ogs are our link to paradise. They don't know evil or jealousy or discontent. To sit with a dog on a hillside on a glorious afternoon is to be back in Eden, where doing nothing was not boring—it was peace.

Milan Kundera

# I took to dogs

It got so I couldn't feel comfortable with folks, not since Mrs. Riddle died, and having no children, and being of a shy nature, I took to dogs. Got so I could train them in a few days. You know, roll over, beg, speak, that sort of thing. Trouble was, I'd get so attached to them I couldn't let them go.

Gerald Green
*Girl*, 1977

# My car dog

**B**ut I wasn't really alone. There was Sam, and he made all the difference. Helen had brought a lot of things into my life and Sam was one of the most precious; he was a beagle and her own personal pet. He would have been about two years old when I first saw him and I had no way of knowing that he was to be my faithful companion, my car dog, my friend who sat by my side through the lonely hours of driving until his life ended at the age of fourteen. He was the first of a series of cherished dogs whose comradeship have warmed and lighted my working life.

James Herriot
*James Herriot's Favorite
Dog Stories*, 1995

# "Chips is here!"

**W**hen I was young, my family lived in Cleveland, and we had a dog named Troubles. Next door was a dog named Chips, and sometimes in the afternoon, when Chips wandered into our yard, my sister would yell, "Troubles! Chips is here! Chips is here!" and Troubles would leap up from wherever she was sleeping and bound into the yard to see her friend. Then we moved away to California, and Troubles got old and cranky and seemed no longer to like other dogs. Chips was still in Cleveland, or dead; we didn't know.

One day my sister had a friend over. They were going through the old photo albums from Cleveland, and my sister was telling stories. "All we had to do," I heard her tell her friend, "was yell, 'Troubles! Chips is here! Chips is here!' and then—" And before she could even finish the story Troubles had leapt into the room once more, barking and jumping and sniffing the air. Something had lasted, in spite of all the time that had passed and the changes she had weathered, the trip cross-country, and the kennel, and the cats. My sister put her hand to her mouth, and tears sprang to her eyes, and like the young enchantress desperate to reverse the powerful incantation she had just naively uttered, she cried out, "Troubles, stop! Stop! Stop!" But it did no good. Nothing would calm Troubles, and nothing would dissuade her, as she barked and jumped and whined and nosed for that miraculous dog who had crossed the years and miles to find her.

David Leavitt
"Chips Is Here"

## The meaning of devotion

He is loyalty itself. He has taught me the meaning of devotion. With him, I know a secret comfort and a private peace. He has brought me understanding where before I was ignorant. His head on my knee can heal my human hurts.

Gene Hill
*Tears & Laughter,* 1997

# In a Quarrel

t night my wife and I did fall out about the dog's being put down in the Sellar, which I had a mind to have done because of his fouling the house, and I would have my will; so we went to bed and lay all night in a Quarrel.

Samuel Pepys
*The Diary of Samuel
Pepys: 1662, 2000*

# The dog outlasted our marriage

The dog outlasted our marriage. He was a large, blond Labrador, the safest, gentlest breed. A family dog who started out as a puppy with too much skin, he turned into an outsized, slightly neurotic giant whom the children adored.

Phyllis Theroux
*California and Other States of Grace:*
*A Memoir,* 1980

# The family dinner table

Y ears and years later, whenever we came back together at the family dinner table, we would start the dog stories. He was the dog who caught the live fish with his mouth, the one who stole a pound of butter off the commissary loading dock and brought it to us in his soft bird dog's mouth without a tooth mark on the package. He was the dog who broke out of Charlie Battery the morning of an ice storm, traveled fourteen miles across the needled grasses and frozen pastures, through the prickly frozen mud of orchards, across backyard fences in small towns, and found the lost family.

Stephanie Vaughn
"Dog Heaven"
*Sweet Talk*, 1990

*When I was a very little lad,*
*I had a very little dog called Punch.*
*I saw to his feeding myself.*

Jack London
"Pictures"
*The Road,* 1907

# A snack between meals

Dandy always had something to eat at mealtimes, but he too liked a snack between meals once or twice a day. The dog biscuits were kept in an open box on the lower dresser shelf, so that he could get one "whenever he felt so disposed," but he didn't like the trouble this arrangement gave him, so he would sit down and start barking, and as he had a bark that was both deep and loud, after it had been repeated a dozen times at intervals of five seconds, any person who happened to be in or near the kitchen was glad to give him his biscuit for the sake of peace and quietness. If no one gave it to him, he would then take it out himself and eat it.

W. H. Hudson
"Dandy, the Story of a Dog"
*A Traveller in Little Things*, 1921

*No animal should jump up on the dining room furniture unless absolutely certain that he can hold his own in the conversation.*

Fran Lebowitz
*Social Studies*, 1977

# Where dogs should sleep

It seems there are two schools of thought holding sharply conflicting theories as to just where dogs should sleep. I myself before I ever had a dog would have repudiated the idea that I would permit one to sleep on my bed, let alone want one to. And the day I brought home a small cocker puppy—still I had no intention of such an arrangement—it was the puppy's own idea, strongly held to. It has turned out through many years to be a good one. Wherever Mickey and I found ourselves, alone in some spooky house I was rebuilding, or in a strange hotel, or in a camping site in the wild sierra, I had only to pat a place near my feet and say, "Lie down, Mickey; it's our home." And it was that for both of us.

Bertha Damon
"Ruffled Paws"

# Just for the pleasure of it

Swimming was his favorite recreation. The first time he ever saw a body of water, he trotted nervously along the steep bank for a while, fell to barking wildly, and finally plunged in from a height of eight feet or more. I shall always remember that shining, virgin dive. Then he swam upstream and back just for the pleasure of it, like a man. It was fun to see him battle upstream against a stiff current, growling every foot of the way. He had as much fun in the water as any person I have ever known. You didn't have to throw a stick into the water to get him to go in. Of course, he would bring back a stick if you did throw one in. He would have brought back a piano if you had thrown one in.

James Thurber
"Snapshot of a Dog"
*The Middle-Aged Man on the Flying Trapeze*, 1933

# Snapshot

I have a snapshot of Joe and me at the Jersey shore. It is 1937 and I am twelve years old; there I am in my bathing suit, grinning, Joe standing on his hind legs with his forepaws in my hands. The top of his beautiful black-and-white head just reaches my skinny chest. It is evident that we are mad about each other.

George Pitcher
*The Dogs Who Came to Stay,* 1995

# Have a pond of water handy

Newfoundland dogs are good to save children from drowning, but you must have a pond of water handy and a child, or else there will be no profit in boarding a Newfoundland.

Josh Billings
*Essays*, c. 1880

# Lassie come-home

There was an old couple in Durham who found a dog lying exhausted in a ditch one night—lying there with its head to the south. They took that dog into their cottage and warmed it and fed it and nursed it. And because it seemed an understanding, wise dog, they kept it in their home, hoping it would be content. But, as it grew stronger, every afternoon toward four o'clock it would go to the door and whine, and then begin pacing back and forth between the door and the window, back and forth as the animals do in their cages at the zoo.

They tried every wile and every kindness to make it bide with them, but finally, when the dog began to refuse food, the old people knew what they must do. Because they understood dogs, they opened the door one afternoon and they watched the collie go, not down the road to the right, or to the left, but straight across a field toward the south, going steadily at a trot, as if he knew he still had a long, long road to travel.

Eric Knight
*Lassie Come-Home,* 1940

# She lived with idiots

L assie looked brilliant, in part because the farm family she lived with was made up of idiots. Remember? One of them was always getting pinned under the tractor, and Lassie was always rushing back to the farmhouse to alert the other ones. She'd whimper and tug at their sleeves, and they'd always waste precious minutes saying things—"Do you think something's wrong? Do you think she wants us to

follow her? What is it, girl?," etc.—as if this had never happened before, instead of every week. What with all the time these people spent pinned under the tractor,

I don't see how they managed to grow any crops whatsoever. They probably got by on federal crop supports, which Lassie filed the applications for.

Dave Barry

# The people the Airedale bit

Mother used to send a box of candy every Christmas to the people the Airedale bit. The list finally contained forty or more names. Nobody could understand why we didn't get rid of the dog. I didn't understand it very well myself, but we didn't get rid of him. I think that one or two people tried to poison Muggs—he acted poisoned once in a while—and old Major Moberly fired at him once with his service revolver near the Seneca Hotel in East Broad Street—but Muggs lived to be almost eleven years old and even when he could hardly get around he bit a congressman who had called to see my father on business. My mother never liked the congressman—she said the signs of his horoscope showed he couldn't be trusted (he was Saturn with the moon in Virgo)—but she sent him a box of candy that Christmas. He sent it right back, probably because he suspected it was trick candy. Mother persuaded herself it was all for the best that the dog had bitten him, even though Father lost an important business association because of it. "I wouldn't be associated with such a man," Mother said. "Muggs could read him like a book."

James Thurber
*My Life and Hard Times*, 1933

# I'm delirious

**A**ny lover of border collies will tell you, and I suppose it may be the same for lovers of any breed, that when you're in the midst of a mob of them, it's like having free run of a theme park, wonders and joyrides every which way you look, a male's parading for a female, one sulks under a chair, two team up to search for a lost toy, one flashes a fang at another. As if at a family reunion joyously cleansed of ill will, I find few things more entertaining than watching border collies interact with each other. I love noting their similarities, their differences, the drama of creating and maintaining a hierarchy. Plus, to me, their distinctive white blaze and ruff is the familiar mark of a beloved beauty—when I see a crowd of them, I'm delirious.

Elisabeth Rose
*For the Love of a Dog: A Memoir,* 2001

# A dachshund named Fred

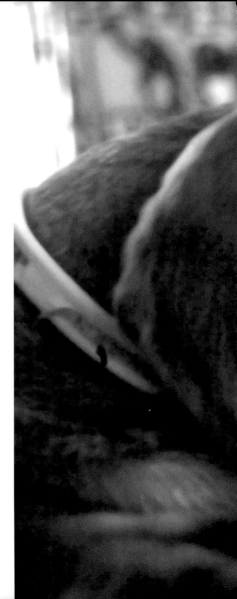

For a number of years past I have been agreeably encumbered by a very large and dissolute dachshund named Fred. Of all the dogs whom I have served I've never known one who understood so much of what I say or held it in such deep contempt. When I address Fred I never have to raise either my voice or my hopes. He even disobeys me when I instruct him in something he wants to do. And when I answer his peremptory scratch at the door and hold the door open for him to walk through, he stops in the middle and lights a cigarette, just to hold me up.

E. B. White
"The Care and Training of a Dog,"
1941

# Begging

The year was 1960 and after having spent every Sunday evening for the past six years watching *Lassie* on television, I desperately wanted a collie. A brilliant, loyal, gentle dog who would follow me around and make me look cool to my friends. Her name would be Lassie, of course, and she could sleep on my bed and help me with my homework.

My mother said collies had too much hair, so we couldn't have one. I explained to her the benefits of dog ownership, and how the compassion I would learn from caring for an animal would make me a better person and contribute to the goal of world peace and interspecies understanding.

Things were not going well. My well-rehearsed speech was replaced by begging, which dissolved into whining. Nothing worked. Collies had too much hair. Case closed.

Next, I tried for an afghan. Afghans were everything I wanted to be: tall, sophisticated, dignified, and thin with long, beautiful, perfect hair, an aloof attitude, and exotic names like Dagmar or Siegfried. I desperately wanted to share my life with an afghan. We would name her Svetlana and she could sleep on my bed and provide me with a constant example of good posture. Again, the hair issue came up. We compromised and settled on a cocker spaniel.

Mary Tiegreen

## Cary Grant

The first love of my life was Cary Grant, a silver-haired miniature poodle. Because the puppy had the most stunning blue eyes, my aunt Hannah had named him after the movie star (and paid the breeder an extra $500). Two weeks after Cary arrived home, his blue eyes turned brown, a trick of nature that my uncle Sol never quite forgave and certainly never forgot.

Linda Sunshine

*Don't accept your dog's admiration as conclusive evidence that you are wonderful.*

Ann Landers

# The dog had business

After spending a petless year with only one child still living at home, my parents visited a breeder and returned with Great Dane they named Melina. They loved this dog in proportion to its size, and soon their hearts had no room for anyone else. In terms of mutual respect and admiration, their six children had been nothing more than a failed experiment. Melina was the real thing. The house was given over to the dog, rooms redecorated to suit her fancy. Enter your former bedroom and you'd be told, "You'd better not let Melina catch you in here," or, "This is where we come to peepee when there's nobody home to let us outside, right, girl!" The knobs on our dresser were whittled down to damp stumps, and our beds were matted with fine, short hairs. Scream at the mangled leather carcass lying at the foot of the stairs, and my parents would roar with laughter. "That's what you get for leaving your wallet on the kitchen table."

The dog was their first genuine common interest, and they loved it equally, each in his or her own way. Our mother's love tended toward the horizontal, a pet being little more than a napping companion, something she could look at and say, "That seems like a good idea. Scoot over, why don't you." A stranger peeking through the window might think that the two of them had entered a suicide pact. She and the dog sprawled like corpses, their limbs arranged in an eternal embrace. "God, that felt good," my mom would say, the two of them waking for a brief scratch. "Now let's go try it on the living room floor."

My father loved the Great Dane for its size, and frequently took her on long, aimless drives, during which she'd stick her heavy, anvil-sized head out the window and leak great quantities of foamy saliva. Other drivers pointed and stared, rolling down their windows to shout, "Hey, you got a saddle for that thing?" When out for a walk there was the inevitable, "Are you walking her, or is it the other way 'round?"

"Ha-ha!" our father always laughed, as if it were the first time he'd heard it. The attention was addictive, and he enjoyed a pride of accomplishment he never felt with any of us. It was as if he were somehow responsible for her beauty and stature, as if he'd personally designed her spots and trained her to grow to the size of a pony. When out with the dog, he carried a leash in one hand and a shovel in the other. "Just in case," he said.

"Just in case, what, she dies of a heart attack and you need to bury her?" I didn't get it.

"No," he said, "the shovel is for, you know, her . . . business."

My father was retired, but the dog had business.

David Sedaris
*Me Talk Pretty One Day*, 2000

# He revered my father

When my parents got their first dog, Tom, they picked him up from a breeder in New Hampshire and took him home in the car, an hour and a half drive. . . . He spent the whole trip curled in my father's coat pocket, and although he always loved my mother, he revered my father after that, in an awestruck, slightly intimidated, approval-coveting way that I understood completely because I shared it.

Caroline Knapp
*Pack of Two*, 1998

# His adoring soul

For it is by muteness that a dog becomes for one so utterly beyond value; with him one is at peace where words play no torturing tricks. When he just sits lovingly and knows that he is being loved, those are the moments that I think are precious to a dog; when, with his adoring soul coming through his eyes, he feels that you are really thinking of him.

John Galsworthy
"Memories," 1924

# I think of him oftenest

A really companionable and indispensable dog is an accident of nature. You can't get it by breeding for it, and you can't buy it with money. It just happens along. Out of the vast sea of assorted dogs that I have had dealings with, by far the noblest, best, and most important was the first, the one my sister sent me in a crate. He was an old-style collie, beautifully marked, with a blunt nose, and great natural gentleness and intelligence. When I got him he was what I badly needed. I think probably all these other dogs of mine have been just a groping toward that old dream. I've never dared get another collie for fear the comparison would be too uncomfortable. I can still see my first dog in all the moods and situations that memory has filed him away in, but I think of him oftenest as he used to be right after breakfast on the back porch, listlessly eating up a dish of petrified oatmeal rather than hurt my feelings. For six years he met me at the same place after school and convoyed me home—a service he thought up himself. A boy doesn't forget that sort of association. It is a monstrous trick of fate that now, settled in the country and with sheep to take care of, I am obliged to do my shepherding with the grotesque and sometimes underhanded assistance of two dachshunds and a wire haired fox terrier.

E. B. White
"The Care and Training of a Dog," 1941

# Staring at the dog

I seem to spend a great deal of time just staring at the dog, struck by how mysterious and beautiful she is to me and by how much my world has changed since she came along.

Caroline Knapp
*Pack of Two*, 1998

# Asking nothing in return

I recommend those persons of either sex, but chiefly, it would seem of mine, whose courage is inclined to fail them if they are long alone, who are frightened in the evenings if there is nobody to speak to, who don't like putting out their own lights and climbing silently to a solitary bedroom, who are full of affection and have nothing to fasten it on to, who long to be loved, and, for whatever reason, aren't—I would recommend all such to go, say, to Harrods, and buy a dog. There, in eager rows, they will find a choice of friends, only waiting to be given the chance of cheering and protecting. Asking nothing in return, either, and, whatever happens, never  going to complain, never going to be cross, never going to judge, and against whom no sin committed will be too great for immediate and joyful forgiveness.

Elizabeth von Arnim
*All the Dogs of My Life,* 1936

# Our house a kennel

O ur house was always filled with dogs. . . .
They helped make our house a kennel, it is
true, but the constant patter of their filthy
paws and the dreadful results of
their brainless activities
have warmed me
throughout the years.

Helen Hayes, with
Sandford Dody
*On Reflection: An
Autobiography,*
1968

## You've always got me

nd when we bury our face in our hands and wish we had never been born, they don't sit up very straight and observe that we have brought it all upon ourselves. They don't even hope it will be a warning to us. But they come up softly, and shove their heads against us. . . . He looks up with his big, true eyes, and says with them, "Well, you've always got me, you know. We'll go through the world together and always stand by each other, won't we?"

Jerome K. Jerome
*Idle Thoughts of an Idle Fellow*, 1889

# Acknowledgements

A big, barking-out-loud, thank you to our wonderful, divine, and ever-attentive editor, Annetta Hanna. She has been our guardian angel on both our Family books and we simply adore her and the delicious Greek lunches we call "editorial meetings."

Thanks to our original booster, Philip Patrick, and to Marysarah Quinn who was immensely helpful to us in pulling this book together. And to dog-loving Maggie

Hinders who carefully groomed this book over so many months and, with us, watched this puppy grow.

Thank you to the folks at Corbis and all the professional photographers who submitted photos for our consideration, especially Dede Hatch, Margaretta Mitchell, Susan Baker, and Polly and Randall Blair.

We love our generous friends who gave us photos of their beloved pets so major kisses and hugs to Susan Dorenter, Marsha Heckman, Sue Wolf, Caroline Beegan, Milbry Polk and Phil Bauman, Bill and Elisabeth Polk, Melinda Barber and Tom Ritchie, Chris Miele and Tony Acosta, Hubert Pedroli, Gemma Antczak, Robin Siegel, and Uncle Bob Goodman whose wonderful photographs contribute so much to this book.

Lastly, we want to thank every dog we have ever known and loved for making our lives more livable.

Linda Sunshine and Mary Tiegreen

*May all the dogs that I have ever loved*
*carry my coffin,*
*howl at the moonless sky,*
*and lie down with me sleeping*
*when I die.*

Erica Jong
"Best Friends"
*At the Edge of the Body,* 1979